IN TIME

IN TIME

Ethel Rackin

THE WORD WORKS
Washington DC

Cover design: Susan Pearce
Cover art: Sarah J. Sloat

ISBN: 978-1-944585-86-0

ACKNOWLEDGMENTS

Grateful acknowledgement is made to the following publications, in which poems from *In Time* first appeared, some in different form:

American Poetry Review: "The Greening," "Homesteaders," "Fire," "Underwood," "Precedent," "Island Life," "New Rules," "Future Lives"

Allium: "7 am," "What Color," "The Mirror Ship, the Painting Teacher, and Me," "January"

Colorado Review: "Something Like Life"

Columbia Poetry Review: "Grandfather Clock," "Ruse," "Deepwater Horizon," "7 pm"

Kestrel: "Silk Road," "Voice Memo: Tanka," "1 pm," "Transfer," "Dawn's Studio," "Painter at Dusk"

The Laurel Review: "Main Street," "Inquiry"

New England Review: "Forge"

One Art: "This Late," "A Solitary Box," "A Way Out," "Sun," "Small Things"

Volt: "Belly"

Thank you to Nancy White for her generous attention. Thank you for the gift of time from MacDowell, where this book was started, and from Bucks County Community College for granting me a sabbatical. Thanks to my colleagues and friends for their support, including Mary Biddinger, Christopher Bursk, Gillian Conoley, Mark Danowsky, John Gallaher, Kasey Jueds, Cecile Kandl, Carolyn Kuebler, Joanne Leva, Carole Maso, Pamela Miller, Randall Potts, Dean Rader, Donald Revell, James Richardson, Hassen Saker, Hayden Saunier, Elizabeth Savage, Elizabeth Scanlon, Sarah J. Sloat, Gerald Stern, Susan Stewart, Tony Trigilio, David Trinidad, and Jenn Un. Love and gratitude to Rebecca Hoenig, Phyllis and Donald Rackin, and Dan Spirer.

For Donald Rackin

(1933-2022)

My True North

CONTENTS

Homecoming

Underwood

Lately

HOMECOMING

THE GREENING

I walked beyond the stone fence, down the
winding road, into a neighbor's yard, and stood
looking into their pool. Where was I headed—
the road seemed a dead-end given the urgency
of everything. The flowers dying violently—stems
truncated from heads—as if they'd never come
back. The pool, the lawn, the fence all shrouded
in shades of green though most of the hues were
sickly holograms of their former selves—or so I
thought. Had I lived long enough to reach back
to a past where it wasn't already happening? By it
I mean the great migration, which none of us could
wrap our heads around, even those who'd
watched their cars float away, their houses burn.
By this time the birds were singing more loudly to
reach each other over the general din, and the sea
of green enveloped me then.

TRANSFER

I tried all the things—
made a book for you, signed, sealed—
carried you across an ocean.
The shirt on my arms
had started to fray—
didn't stop
to mend it—
probably unmendable.
I simply carried my body
to where you were sunning
and lay myself down.
In this way—
I told myself—
I could be your lifeboat
a ship for you to sail
those dark waters
we seemed to inhabit.

AT THE BEGINNING

I was solitary—
gradually time passed—
those were years
depending
on your vantage
no more
than
a feather's
weight.

THANKS

for your call.
The hydrangeas here are lovely
as you—the caller—are lovely.
I'm sitting in the garden
such as it is—
more a weedy vineland
than a garden—
thinking of you
the nature of loss.
Things grow, you lose them.
Meanwhile, Mary Ruefle's helpful.
Thank you for your menopause poem
Mary Ruefle.
Thank you for having a name
that reminds me of a cake flower.

CAFÉ WINDOW

Two women take pictures
of their daughters in hats—
one blonde, one brunette
like their mothers—
two mothers in the window
taking pictures—one blonde—
in hats of the same size—
taking pictures—moving
in two hats—
daughters in the window
now seated without
mothers in pictures.

BELLY

It's my second
home, I explain

~

Where's *my* RV
asks Mother—

I want
one

~

Your mother's the one
who always rubbed
your belly
when you were sick
the healer explained

~

That description
always stuck

~

No
matter
what

CERISE

A terribly round wound or womb
word—my world—spinning
this green glassy spinning
this cold delicious frightening
this pain of random source
name yourself—I say to the pain—
the pain answers *nil.*

BEECH TREE

You should just be doing nothing
writes my supportive
older male friend.
This much is true—
if I touch the tree
the tree touches me.
Its bark bears the marks
of age, abuse, imperfection—
its healing rub.

WE WALK UNDER

the cherry blossoms
you are old—I am
in the middle—offering
me no advice what
is implied—
not long before I waited
for you in the park
no longer carrying any
ulterior motive
a day like the one
in the atelier—
the blonde girl saying
my boyfriend and I
share the same
temperament
or the couple honking
smiling as we lean
into each other
as we sit on a curb—
and now it's you driving
around this small town
shouting out the car
window—insisting I do
the same—which I never
could.

THE TORTOISE

What did I want to do when I came back
to write—to detail the drift—two wild hares
a dead mouse, a tiny beautiful owl
one of the hares chewed up and now this—
a tortoise's muddy back—what good
what good were those early harbingers—
fragility, death—given my helplessness
while all along the tortoise was somewhere
but where in the absence of visible water
except for run-off. The road's ditch.

HOMECOMING

You run and as you run
you think of Philadelphia—
warm toes—a breeze finally
after so much density
so much rain
the heaviness you feel
in your abdomen
not cancer this time
thankfully not
this time—your time—
as a family of squirrels
or finches
a family of starlings
or larks
sets up shop—in almost
ceaseless effort—if
only you knew.

DAWN'S STUDIO

for Dawn Clements

In various spaces
there are lamps
and in some of them
so many shadows
at times betrayed
by an edge—where one piece
of paper meets another
—sutured—
when you can't stand
you can draw from bed
you can draw your own arm
and the ceiling
eventually a pattern
and words are a part of this pattern—
medical or otherwise—the stage
determines the treatment
develops into your life
from the head down
most minute wrapping
pile of leaves
that grows by day:
see vegetation shifting
observe the edges
of strawberry leaves
if you look long enough
become radiant!

HOMESTEADERS

A couple of years
later, we would set up
our own camp. But for
now, we'd try the idea
on others, testing
to see what kind of
audience we had.
Could we count on
them? We never knew
and things could
change, sometimes all
of a sudden. That's
how I learned
about exorcising
certain creatures.
About opening the
doors for them to
roam. The creatures
came in every size and
shape, but snakes
were especially
prevalent as were
alligators. After the
last flooding, the
alligators took over
swimming around

making certain cities
almost uninhabitable.
We took up residence
on one of the few
islands left and
started from scratch.
Our place didn't look
like much. There
wasn't a war around
us though there were
plenty of them. We
simply settled
ridiculous disputes
each and every day
then passed out. After
we had accumulated
enough mantras, we
returned to a feeling of
goodness. The whole
truth was again
accessible.

RECOVERED DAILIES

9/18/18

up at 5 am
well this is the first
crashed the car
lost phone
marooned
on this island
      what will
I write   well
it's another day

~

it's starting to rain
where are my
rain boots
      why would it
be any different

9/19/18

my feet on the ground
my lumps and pains
my feet on the ground

9/20/18

found sparrows
in my chest
this morning—
a golden penny
what more can I offer
a trace of what
I was

9/21/18

what you find
may be worthwhile
said the earth-
worm to the frog
and in this way
life distilled—
stilled

9/22/18

in this now
that is us listening—
to stop from falling
and peeking
through leaves
now that we are separate pieces
stocked back
into the kind of trouble
we earlier feared
how can I be here
and this branching
into nothing

9/23/18

the prow of a ship
now leading—

boy with a sail
girl with the sun

fall's
whirl

9/29/18

chalk it up
to too much coffee

fall weather
weather's undeniable
drift shine
shine drift

craft it out of sheer
intention
craft it out of sullen
shyness

this is your time
to lose

FORGE

Forge a temporary structure for feed—for nesting
for things you'll lose along the way—
the highway from here to Missoula
from here to Lubbock—from sea to—
pack a roll-out, a canister for tears
record your dreams and take note
of sounds and scents around you
forgive your mother her trespasses
your loves the pain they've inflicted
friends their betrayals and disappointments
befriend small animals and children
form groups—call frequently—rather
than texting. Make an appointment
with loss—with griefs you didn't know
you had—with lumps you're too afraid
to discover. Attempt to start a fire—
use sticks for this. Sit on a pelt atop
the cold firm ground. Remember
the animals in your dreams—
you may need them later.
Place your loved ones'
pictures in a locket
traverse forests
learn to see in the woods
at night without a flashlight.
Learn to cook over an open flame—

almost anything—nettles, berries, bits
of dandelion leaves. There will not always
be meat. There will not always be adequate shelter.
There will not always be water.
There will not always be string.

UNDERWOOD

FIRE

Before paper became a rare commodity.
Before the need arose to go anywhere
to put on anything special
there was a longing in me that
would not be named. There was
a lion breaking free and a child
who kept caging him. By this
I don't mean I was unhappy
especially since happiness
seemed difficult to define
only that I wanted something and
couldn't be sure of its whereabouts
or how to capture it. Sidelined—
waiting for a better time. That's
how the need developed. If I just
waited long enough, I too, even
in my shortest, most female form
would somehow, as they say, emerge.
Now I see that emergence carries
with its root multiple associations
with water—including from
the Latin *mergere*: to plunge—
and that it takes a needful wish
to plunge or burn through
whatever it is that keeps us
from being alive.

UNDERWOOD

It was an ordinary day—we were running
errands. As far as I was concerned, all
was well, or so I said, except for the
worry (almost relentless), except for the way
everyone seemed to stare and either hold
their breath or exhale their venom all over
each other on the daily. There was the guy
who signaled to hurry up. The woman who
screamed at me for not putting up enough signs.
Who left you event police, I wanted to scream back
but I bit my lip and gnashed my terrible
teeth and tried not to become a wild thing.
This wasn't patience, my teacher reminded me.
I'd have to lean in further for that. I'd
have to be able to truly welcome the stranger
as one of my kind mothers, as one of my own.

BELATED

There was no need yet to start packing
my bags. The sky I remembered was still
the sky. The stars aligned on a clear night
though you would hear the distant cries
of animals and couldn't be sure they were
actually there. The meat had different names.
The produce was gigantic, brightly colored, and
came with labels to remind you of the taste
and smell (they hadn't yet been perfected).
Dogs who weren't mine had joined my pack
and I couldn't tell them apart.
It turned out I needed both dogs and people—
all of them. I needed them to get out of there.
I gave money—what was left of it—to an old
acquaintance fighting cancer. The family
didn't want the strays when I tried to return them.
By the time I made it to the party, I had fashioned
myself in layers. I'd gathered my dogs, my other things.
I could think of no place I'd rather be and
the mood was triumphant, except for
a feeling I was leaving it all behind.

ESPLANADE

You speak to me that way—
now a separate mountain, now
a forest, now through the wind
whispering down trunks of trees.
I spot you in candy wrappers
in magnets, in blankets I keep
and threadbare ones I give away.
If I wanted to find the one we shared
now that I've given it to the thrift store
across the road, around the corner
how would I find it? What would I
say to the volunteer, the cashier?
That I want my blanket back
because it reminds me of you?

MAIN STREET

There were things I just had to survive—
shiny things in my heart—

they were personal until they weren't
because they burst onto the scene—singing—

made their way onto subway platforms, boxcars
kept on going even after the lights went out

in my house and on porches
all over America—

things so small
they must have been imagined

but now we're here
standing out in the rain

what is it we seek
and whom have we come to know—knocking.

GRANDFATHER CLOCK

Walking around like this
a good book in my hands
the dead letter office
E.D.'s envelope poems
my organs—mostly—intact
we are all political now
says a man with a conscience—
not my president—
ties for things like this
fruit stands in the rain
enlarged hearts.

SILK ROAD

In the burnished tree
what cold branches
now stare down
affixed
with the last of snow

for winter's just a metaphor
for the kind of loss
we figure on—
forgive me

friends.

SIGNS

We could wish them away
tell ourselves
not that horrible
only in numbers that small
even the outraged among us
suspected a certain amount
of hysteria—though
signs were everywhere
everywhere we walked—signs.

PRECEDENT

I wanted something in my heart like a drum.
Peaches fell from trees.
Suddenly: monsoon season.
So, I told myself a story
to soothe myself into a kind of slumber
not like the wrestling recently begun
not like the wager life seems hell-bent
on becoming. Meanwhile, my friends
I've meant to call you—all around trees
collapsing, arterial roads blocked
then blocked again. The country
seems triply damned. The old
precedents mean nothing.

INQUIRY

My mother thinks democratic liberalism's
run its course and she's probably right.
Can we think our way through grit
through the tooth achy reality?
Reality tv started what befalls us now.
I point my finger and my point's lost.
This is the night I start all of my poems—
the first's a lullaby—*shhh*—the next's on fire
but no one's listening, sees it burning.
Lost names, missing table, place to defecate—
it's not me but it will be soon.
Am I going to start gathering my things
and will my patience practice protect me?
I mean, at least it's a way of thinking.

RUSE

You would make up some story
each of us would come close
to repeating
between headlines—
an ocean of lies—really—
close to out of luck
for those of us
left standing.

DEEPWATER HORIZON

It's easy to see
what stands between us—
me and the orange sun—
for who owns the sun
who owns the sea?
Well, in a sense, BP
does—the company
I mean country.

VOICE MEMO: TANKA

Morning spectator
I wrote from a dense forest
I wrote from a lake
in my heart—I called the waves
the waves in my glove-like heart.

ISLAND LIFE

While we were in prison we kept staring at each other
and telling our stories of miraculous things
that had happened to us before this befell us.
We kept ourselves alive this way—recounting the exact sounds
the flora and fauna, the colors of each variety of sea
lichen and numbering species almost as if
we were creating a catalogue of tears. This too
played with our minds, which is to say
we still weren't sure which speculative future we'd
invested ourselves into and why, of all places
we would have wanted to end up in
maximum security. Had we needed protection?
(Not that we were really protected.) Had we
finished all the novels that had fallen
by this time into the sea? Meanwhile, one of us
noticed a couple of old-timey suitcases piled
up in a corner of our cell. How was this possible?
I wanted to start memorizing every detail then
to form some kind of trying. I wanted to stay living.

NEW RULES

And where was I on the new rules
which side would I come down on
I guess I was annoyed
like any animal who has to work
to keep bones in the refrigerator
and pick up so many things each
and every day
and sulked because there was never enough
to write my field notes uninterrupted
or dream my dreams
and wondering if I had the new variant
and whether I'd communicate it to my parents
I stored these thoughts deep in cells
for fear that fear would take me over
and like any animal alive on this planet
felt it in my glands, but knowing
how good I had it compared to so many
others I dreamed my dream and slept
that fabulous sleep and wrote out
of a sense of loss but also a sense of glee
whether or not these were truly the end times
as many seemed to think they were
and here I was at this miraculous moment
in my pajamas, almost fifty, and in goodly shape
except for the hidden things my spine spoke of
except for the far reaches.

FUTURE SELVES

The women were just like me, except they weren't.
They wore their hair adorned, their jeans.
Each of us used to come to this theater
before it and everything around it closed
before the bike shop and candle shop and bakery
all closed down due to too much population
or never enough. Whichever it was, I remembered
that time fondly. I remembered going out
among the crowds and lights. The looks I got
and what I looked at. By this
you should not conclude I'm lonely.
Days pass almost unrecognizably
and there are so many entertainments. I am
not the bored housewife I was once nor am I
the overworked teacher or the frustrated
writer. I'm not the painting hobbyist
the short woman with a mostly strong body
in all kinds of pain. I'm not the student
in love. Since all these selves have been purged
I'm better off, you could say. I can complete
the real assignment.

VISITS

8 PM

You can't control winter
you can't control cancer

publication, the cost of things
how much you'll strain.

Meanwhile, the library's waiting
and stars align over an endless bridge

of becoming (forgetting)
as cold milk swims in a tall glass

under the porch's automatic light.
It will come on, you know

it will come on

in case you don't
remember.

7 AM

It was not yet time to put on the cloak
that would keep her warm
hibiscus still opening and
seemingly on each side
but as for the turning of flowers
really, it was anybody's guess.

7 *PM*

A poet visits
as glamorous
as rain—right
as rain—you think
in all the different
ways—where are
my socks—where
is that gloss I used
to wear?

5 AM

This much
is true—you open
the door, the big dog
roams, a breeze
whips up—
the day's neither dark
nor light. There's found
money in it.

6 AM

Applebutter Road, it's
ugly on the face of it
still something quiet inside—
a dog softly rising
the ritual grey or green
in which dreams soak
or float.

1 *PM*

You're absolutely perfect
she said to the dog, the goat
the bee—
the last you'd expect
to shine—
and in this way
she became me.

5 PM

for Carole Maso

After re-reading *Ava*
A Novel of Thank You
Break All the Rules
so much thanks

thanks to be safe

your Rose is lovely
someday you'll meet
my Daffodil
not big as Basket

save me a place
at your table
this Christmas Eve

just beginning

dusk arriving out
the windows
soon we'll light
Hanukkah candles

our first year
can you imagine
two Jews
not celebrating

all this holiday
time passes
yours and Woolf's

then there's
the in-between
of late afternoon
arrivals

for this
my friend
thank you

Noon

For Arnold Markley

I liked how I could look
from one room of my house to the other.

The outside view was always obstructed
but I didn't mind, or maybe I did.

The sun shone on the dog's fur
when she sat in exactly the right spot

but was it really alright for her—
the fur, the sun?

So many things arrived wrapped
like gifts

though the moment I apprehended them
they seemed to disappear.

One was a letter from you—
spelling out every last intention—

the hymns, psalms and poems
the order of the procession—

maybe it was finally possible
to beckon you back in

but only long enough
to lose you once again.

LATELY

THIS LATE

in the day
the sky's thirsty tilting
staring down on us—
all of it—the drinks—drunk—
as you and I might slip
into the kind of trance
we were in
at the beginning
if we're not careful
if it's still possible:

DREAM JOURNAL

I have lost both my legs—
replaced by metal ones.
I can still move—
it's almost as if nothing
has happened.

~

I can go into the woods
with a fervor to forget
or forget about the fervor.
The woods are not metaphorical—
you can see through them on one side
and I'm listening and trying hard to forget
and trudging through deep leaves
or swimming through cloudy sludge.
Some days it's enough just to survive.

~

She offers me fruit
and reaching to take starfruit from the top of the plate
I am punished—she rescinds the plate
serving herself the best first
for me only berries—
this continues all winter
in my mind
on paper—in dreams.

~

We have gone somewhere tropical
after many hard months
and I am desirous
as I haven't been in a long time
I feel myself opening to you
wanting to take you in public
not so that we can be seen
but because I'm ready
I wake wanting you.

A SOLITARY BOX

is arranged.
To you it's just
a box
but to me it holds
so much
forgiveness.

A WAY OUT

The shells you wear you
withdraw into—
by staying motionless
you prepare
a temporary explosion—
not to say whirlwind—
it's in your nature.

SUN

Someday you'll rise
and face the sun
head into the hills—
your heart's interest—
nearly stunning
in your vicissitudes
you'll shun that sun
shadow.

MACDOWELL WOODS

for Gerald Stern

Through the day
all I could hear was howling—
or was it crying—
or was it all through the night
that fall into winter
something inside was breaking
or was it writhing—rising—writing—
righting itself against the night?
Some nights I heard it
and called it by your name—
Jerry, I wondered
when will I know?
Some nights it was close
to a whisper
to the shared laughter
say, of a sister
and every day after that
ceaselessly listening.

FAMILIAL

When you are gone, I will think it is the beach
that makes me miss you, but it won't be the beach.
I will think it is days together under the hot sun
but it won't be the sun. I will think it is the faded umbrella
the keys left, the cottage door. I will think it is the cottage
but it won't be the cottage. It was never that old wooden door.
You are the *I* I've always known, the I that sometimes wakes at night,
aches for home, returns remembering
so little. Am I the *you* you'd imagined I'd be at this age—
almost the age your mother died, suddenly
one hot summer night? Am I that Ethel for you
just as you are Mom according to us alone—
our one and only mother—though surely
there've been others, surely we've known
each other before?

PAINTER AT DUSK

I've got my stars
I've got my map—
a tourist's map is all—
I've got my keys
I've got my fur—
fur, spirit and all!

~

I've got my carrying case
I've got my valise—
a map of stars is all.
A star-flecked horse
a can of juice
Homer's lost
and paintings
grow dark.

~

A damasked map
of stars is all
and all is lost
bliss.

~

Slipping into the wine-dark sea
days of drafts
a pile of dross.

~

That drug will drag you
into the flecked sea
as swallows die
whose whittled sea is lost.

THE MIRROR SHIP

By the time we got there
the Mirror Ship had landed
in all its untold beauty. You
were beside yourself, meaning next
to me. It was winter. I could tell
because the berries on the trees
were plump in their redness, or so
my painting teacher claimed. She was
the kind of witch who would praise
you one day and tell you you had
muffin top the next. What did this
tell us about the Mirror Ship? Did
the painting teacher's unavoidable tic
have anything to do with me, my mind
where I was standing at the time, the future
the price of trees this year? Yes, yes
and yes…I couldn't stand it any
longer. I decided to begin again
only as one memory, one immutable
perception, endlessly moving.

JANUARY

To say I felt a loss wasn't exactly it.
It's just that a wind blew
and I wasn't sure where it was
coming from. Several tall candles stood
unlit. A piece of land left undeveloped.
Who would buy it? Would they use it
to raise donkeys, horses, cows? None
of the neighbors could be sure.
Meanwhile, we had to get up
each day, put on our socks and
other things, go to work, and pretend
not to think about any of it. The
more we pretended, the more it felt
real.

SMALL THINGS

get to you
wherever you are you are
whether or not you leave
you leave—
this flowering triangle
will come to nothing
if you're not steadfast
or true. Be the wind
in sail. All precious
metals.

WHAT COLOR

will the waves be when you finally see them—
the same as always, the same as always.

SOMETHING LIKE LIFE

There was a window—
in it many leaves moved
many moons arose
new poems
rose-colored leaves
eventually falling
in piles of prayers.
Snow fell too
inside the frame
of that window—
museum of white—
while I waited
for something to be lifted—
something like life—
for a path to be cleared
though it was not yet winter—
trees shone (as they do now)
I can attest to much celebration
I can attest to endless wind rustling—
to that great show of light coming through.

SOI-DISANT

Your whole body—
its Zenith so bright—
your wake nearly
blinding—

are you getting to the point yet—
moving out against the sun?

NAUSICAÄ

There's heart
shelter
an amber anchor
even in weather
for you have good shoulders
though the bees you flick
come back.

LATELY

I have the feeling—
this way of living—
I'm talking about luck here
though I don't mean to say
a single day arrives
for it's been my experience
things come up
disaster stops the tracks
for each life lived—
forgive—
feels like awe
feels like all.

ABOUT THE AUTHOR

Ethel Rackin is the author of three other collections: *The Forever Notes* (Parlor Press, 2013); *Go On* (Parlor Press, 2016), a National Jewish Book Award finalist; and *Evening* (Furniture Press, 2017). She is also the author of the text *Crafting Poems and Stories: A Guide to Creative Writing* (Broadview Press, 2022).

Her collaborative lyric sequence, "Soledad," written with Elizabeth Savage, was awarded the 2016 Thomas Merton Prize for Poetry of the Sacred by Elizabeth Robinson, and another collaborative sequence, "Silent e," is included in *They Said: A Multi-Genre Anthology of Collaborative Writing* (Black Lawrence Press, 2018). Her work has appeared in *The American Poetry Review*, *Colorado Review*, *Jacket2*, *Kenyon Review*, *New England Review*, *Poetry Daily*, *Verse Daily*, *Volt*, and elsewhere.

She earned her MFA from Bard College and her PhD in English Literature from Princeton University. A MacDowell fellow, she has taught at Penn State Brandywine, Haverford College, and Bucks County Community College in Pennsylvania, where she is a professor of English.

ABOUT THE ARTIST

Sarah J. Sloat is a (visual) poet and the author of *Classic Crimes* and *Hotel Almighty*, both from Sarabande Books. Originally from New Jersey, Sarah has lived in Europe for many years. Her poems, prose and collage have appeared in *The Offing*, *Diagram*, and *Court Green*, among other journals.

ABOUT THE WORD WORKS

Since its founding in 1974, The Word Works has steadily published volumes of contemporary poetry and presented public programs. Its imprints include The Washington Prize, The Tenth Gate Prize, The Hilary Tham Capital Collection, and International Editions.

Monthly, The Word Works offers free programs in its Café Muse Literary Salon. Starting in 2023, the winners of the Jacklyn Potter Young Poets Competition will be presented in the June Café Muse program.

As a 501(c)3 organization, The Word Works has received awards from the National Endowment for the Arts, the National Endowment for the Humanities, the D.C. Commission on the Arts & Humanities, the Witter Bynner Foundation, Poets & Writers, The Writer's Center, Bell Atlantic, the David G. Taft Foundation, and others, including many generous private patrons.

An archive of artistic and administrative materials in the Washington Writing Archive is housed in the George Washington University Gelman Library. The Word Works is a member of the Community of Literary Magazines and Presses.

wordworksbooks.org

OTHER WORD WORKS BOOKS

Annik Adey-Babinski, *Okay Cool No Smoking Love Pony*

Karren L. Alenier, *From the Belly: Poets Respond to Gerturude Stein's Tender Buttons* (ed.) / *Wandering on the Outside*

Nathalie Anderson, *Rough*

Emily August, *The Punishments Must Be a School*

Jennifer Barber, *The Sliding Boat Our Bodies Made*

Andrea Carter Brown, *September 12*

Willa Carroll, *Nerve Chorus*

Grace Cavalieri, *Creature Comforts* / *The Long Game: Poems Selected & New*

Abby Chew, *A Bear Approaches from the Sky*

Nadia Colburn, *The High Shelf*

Henry Crawford, *The Binary Planet*

Barbara Goldberg, *Berta Broadfoot and Pepin the Short* / *Breaking & Entering: New and Selected Poems*

Akua Lezli Hope, *Them Gone*

Michael Klein, *The Early Minutes of Without: Poems Selected & New*

Deborah Kuan, *Women on the Moon*

Frannie Lindsay, *If Mercy*

Elaine Magarrell, *The Madness of Chefs*

Chloe Martinez, *Ten Thousand Selves*

Marilyn McCabe, *Glass Factory*

JoAnne McFarland, *Identifying the Body*

Leslie McGrath, *Feminists Are Passing from Our Lives*

Kevin McLellan, *Ornitheology*

Ron Mohring, *The Boy Who Reads in the Trees*

A. Molotkov, *Future Symptoms*

Ann Pelletier, *Letter That Never*

W. T. Pfefferle, *My Coolest Shirt*

Ayaz Pirani, *Happy You Are Here*

Robert Sargent, *Aspects of a Southern Story* / *A Woman from Memphis*

Roger Smith, *Radiation Machine Gun Funk*

Jeddie Sophronius, *Love & Sambal*

Julia Story, *Spinster for Hire*

Maria Terrone, *No Known Coordinates*

Leah Umansky, *Of Tyrant*

Barbara Ungar, *After Naming the Animals*
Cheryl Clark Vermeulen, *They Can Take It Out*
Julie Marie Wade, *Skirted*
Miles Waggener, *Superstition Freeway*
Fritz Ward, *Tsunami Diorama*
Camille-Yvette Welsch, *The Four Ugliest Children in Christendom*
Amber West, *Hen & God*
Maceo Whitaker, *Narco Farm*

www.ingramcontent.com/pod-product-compliance
Lightning Source LLC
Chambersburg PA
CBHW020322090426
42735CB00009B/1366